Fort Montgomery
Through the years

A Pictorial History of the Great Stone Fort
on Lake Champlain

By James P. Millard

Photo courtesy of Charles Barney

America's Historic Lakes
P.O. Box 262
South Hero, Vermont 05486

Fort Montgomery: Through the years

A Pictorial History of the Great Stone Fort on Lake Champlain

Copyright © 2005 by James P. Millard

Published by

America's Historic Lakes
580 West Shore Road, P.O. Box 262
South Hero, Vermont 05486
http://www.historiclakes.org

ISBN Number 0-9749854-2-2
Printed in the United States of America

Table of Contents

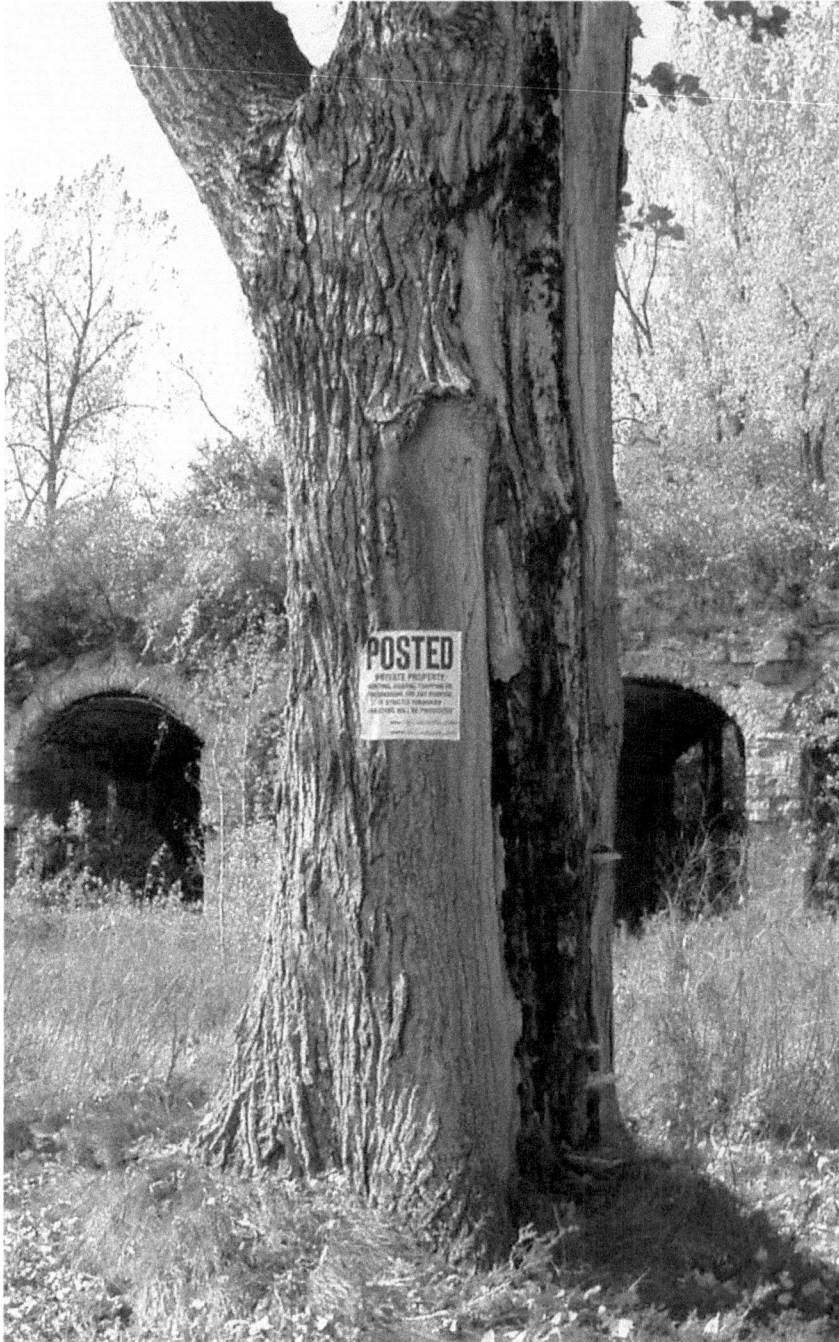

Fort Montgomery is privately owned and the grounds are posted. Please respect the property owners and do not trespass on the grounds of the fort.

Acknowledgements

When I started America's Historic Lakes in 1997 one of the significant questions for me was which locations I should feature prominently. The big, well-known names were obvious. Yet, I wanted this new venture to tell the whole story, give the big picture, to share the remarkable stories of not only the prominent and famous, but the obscure and difficult to get to locations on these storied waterways.

Crab Island became one of those locations, Fort Montgomery was another. Before long, the old ruins in Rouses Point became one of the most asked about places on the site. It was only a matter of time before I realized that with Fort Montgomery, as with Crab Island, a book was also needed.

That undertaking was to prove more challenging than I'd imagined.

A few factors hindered my efforts. First, the body of work about the fort- there really wasn't any. What was available was invaluable- Rev. Daniel Taylor was very proud of the great new fort in his town, and he wrote glowingly about it. I doubt I could have done this book (or the next one) without Taylor's work. Much later, John Ross devoted much time and effort to the fort. His efforts also, have benefited me enormously. Other than these two men, however, few have chosen to write about Fort Montgomery except in a general way.

This book is not meant to be a comprehensive treatment of the fortifications at Rouses Point. That book is in the works and will be for some time yet. This volume is meant to share some of the priceless photographs that have been so generously shared with me over the last few years. Many of the donors are elderly; people who have fond memories of the fort, even before it was demolished in 1936-37. They have graciously shared their images with me for publication; photographic images and mental images- each invaluable and of interest and importance.

These images have been sent to me from across America. Yes, many came from the archives of the Clinton County Historical Association in Plattsburgh. Some came from library special collections and National Archives. This effort would not be complete without their important contributions. Others, however, arrived in my inbox and my mailbox from far away places. Tia Hollowood sent some lovely photos from Alaska as a gift. They will end up wherever my papers do some day.

Raymond Sequin has shared many wonderful images from his home in Florida. He was prompted to do so by Ruth Sequin, his sister, still a local resident. His son Brian assisted in the digitization of many of these important photos.

My good friend Charlie Barney has been a major contributor. Living with his family in the Buffalo area, Charlie is a Rouses Point native whose father, the late Charles Barney, was a long-time law enforcement officer in the town. Charles Senior obviously loved the old structure (a common sentiment). He took many photos before and after its demolition. I am grateful and honored to be able to share those priceless images here.

I could never have taken on this project had I not had the cooperation and trust of Stephen and Victor Podd, current owners of the fort through Fort Montgomery Estates. Stephen and Victor have granted me the privilege of access to the grounds for my research. They have also generously shared with me photos and other items from the personal collection of their father, the late Victor Podd.

I am also very grateful to Ann Thurber. Ann has generously given of her time and she has gone out of her way to provide me with important research materials. Noted Third-System authority John Weaver flew in from Indiana to tour the fort with me and share his knowledge of these great structures. My correspondences with John and his visit have proven very useful indeed.

I am grateful to Clinton County Historian Addie Shields, Ralph Gilpin, Robert Fraser Farnsworth, Judy Swink, and the Clinton County Historical Association for their willingness to share images from their collections. I also thank Donna Racine for spending an afternoon with me sharing her knowledge of Rouses Point history.

I very much want to thank my dear friend and colleague Roger Harwood. Roger has been at my side on almost every trip to the fort. He has taken on the cause of Fort Montgomery and, as I would expect, he is making a difference. In addition to being an untiring researcher, Roger has provided me with immeasurable support and assistance. This book would not have happened without Roger's help. I'm also very grateful to Doug Harwood, Roger's brother. The wonderful aerial photos in the book would not be here without the generosity of Doug Harwood.

Finally, I want to acknowledge the love of my life, my anchor; my dear wife Lynn. Without her patience, support and love I would not be writing these words, the America's Historic Lakes project would not exist.

Introduction

A local resident enters Fort Montgomery through an embrasure in the moat. Clinton County Historical Association photo.

"Fort Montgomery—not a Blunder"… That is the title of an unpublished manuscript in my possession by the late John Ross. Mr. Ross, it seems experienced the same frustrations as this writer with the many misconceptions about the old fort that today stands in ruins just south of the border at Rouses Point.

Of course, there was a Fort "Blunder". It justifiably lives on in local legend. And, it was located here, at Island Point. All traces of it were gone, however, shortly after work on the great stone fortress known properly as Fort Montgomery began.

This book is not about Fort "Blunder'. Readers desiring to know of the first fortification built here in 1816 will need to wait until my next book is available. That volume will be a comprehensive look at all of the fortifications in the Rouses Point area.

And yet, despite its fame, Fort Blunder was but a shadow of the great stone structure built here between 1844 and 1870. This book is about that second fort, one named in honor of General Richard Montgomery, hero of the American Revolution.

The fact that Fort Montgomery was ever built is a testament to the importance of the Lake Champlain/Lake George/Richelieu River corridor. Begun well after the ratification of the Treaty of Ghent in 1815, this treaty effectively brought to an end the War of 1812. It did not bring to a conclusion fear and suspicion between the two nations. The northern frontier between British Canada and the United States would be a source of contention for many years hence. Too many military incursions had taken place on this strategic waterway by both sides to leave the outlet of the lake unprotected.

So it was in the summer of 1844 that clearing was begun and piles were driven for a massive new work on the site of the original unnamed fort recently recovered from Canada by treaty.

Though not technically a part of the "Permanent System of Fortifications" because it was constructed on the northern frontier, this great stone fort bore all the hallmarks of a "permanent" or Third-System fort. The massive stone bastions protruding from the octagonal trace at five locations, the impressive masonry casemates, powder magazines, spiral staircases; all these features and more were found in the smallest and greatest of Chief Engineer Joseph G. Totten's "Permanent System" forts. Despite the fact that construction was carried on in spurts over a thirty-year period, no expense was spared in its design and construction. The Rouses Point location was simply too important.

Fort Montgomery was constructed of limestone, or "black marble" from quarries on Isle la Motte and King's Bay and a lot of brick. The entire fort exterior, scarp walls on every curtain and bastion, was finished with limestone. Yet, a phenomenal amount of brick was used in construction also, a fact not readily known. Brick was used in the massive supporting arches, in the embrasures, and in all of the quarters and storerooms within the fort. This brick was very appealing to the locals, and, once the fort was thought to be abandoned, it was removed in astonishing quantities.

Fort Montgomery has been referred to as "Fort Blunder" due to misinformation about the first fort; it has also been dubbed a "blunder" in the sense that some believe it never should have been constructed. This writer does not believe building the great stone fort at Rouses Point was a mistake, nor was it a symbol of government waste and mismanagement of funds. For far too long the Richelieu River and Lake Champlain had served as an important pathway to invasion. Though almost unimaginable today, relations with Great Britain never really improved much until well after the Civil War. Fort Montgomery served a noble purpose indeed; it was a deterrent to war, a purpose it served very well. Despite published statements to the contrary, the fort was armed. In 1872 there were 72 guns mounted *en casemate* and *en barbette*, well more than half of its planned full complement of 125 guns. These mighty guns were the most successful weapons of all- they were never fired in anger.

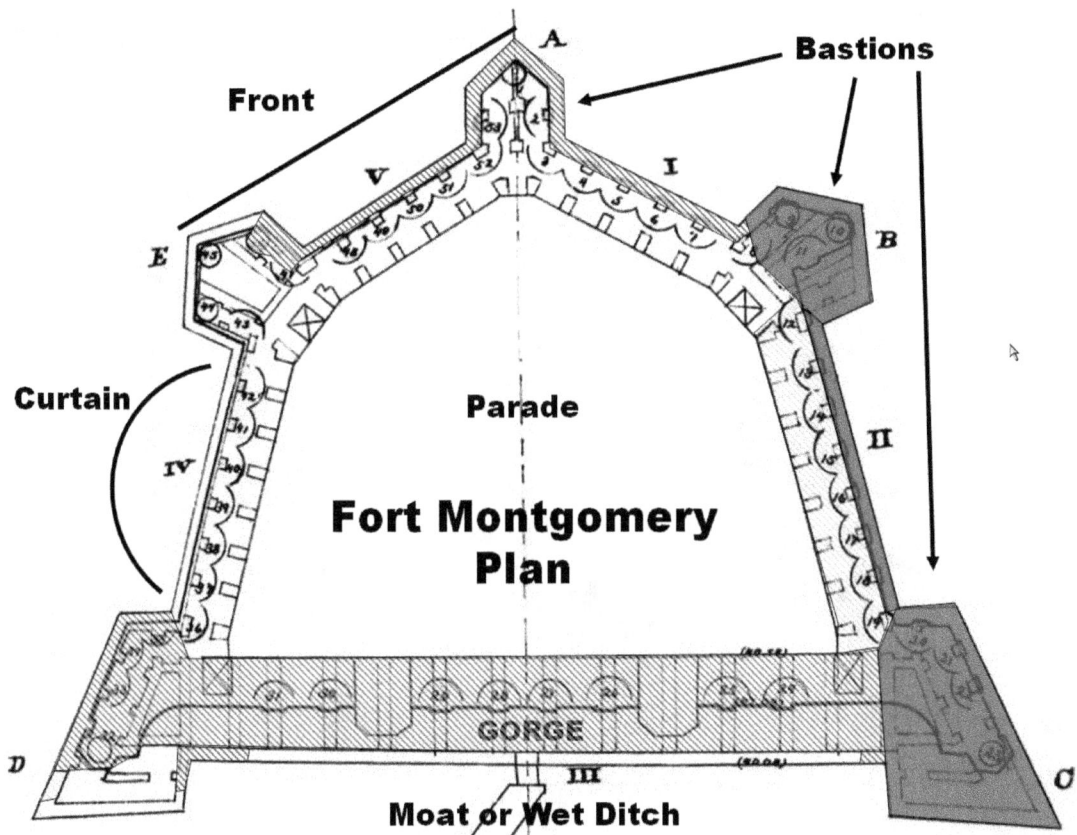

Fort Montgomery Plan

Labels: Front, Bastions, Curtain, Parade, Moat or Wet Ditch, GORGE

This plan of Fort Montgomery has been modified to show Third-System features and terms used throughout this book. The bastions and curtains are identified in the same way they are referred to in official Engineers documents.

The shading shows the various states of the ruins. The darkest shading on Front II identifies the part of the ruins most intact and recognizable. Horizontal shading indicates ruins still standing but badly damaged. Vertical shading reflects areas with some trace of the original structure visible but largely destroyed. Areas with no shading have been completely demolished.

Courtesy of Roger and Doug Harwood.

Courtesy of Robert Fraser Farnsworth

Two aerials views: One spring 1920, the other spring 2005. See Chapter XI for more aerial photographs.

I. Fort Walls- Exterior Views

Fort Montgomery was built to withstand fire from the most powerful guns in use at the time. By the time it was nearly complete some thirty years after it was begun, the advent of rifled cannons caused military planners concern. The Civil War had shown that masonry walls would not stand up to a prolonged battering by high-velocity rifled cannon.

Since the fort was constructed over such a long period, advances in technology were incorporated as the work progressed. Among the most visible changes are the cannon embrasures. Embrasures were among the most vulnerable locations in a fort. Hence, every precaution was taken to protect the gun crews within. The lower tiers were built of hardened brick, while the later embrasures were constructed of masonry reinforced with 3 thick iron bands. These stone walls served one purpose- to protect the guns and the crews manning them. Standing within a casemated battery it is easy to see why a gun crew would prefer to work behind one of the latter embrasures.

Like several other Third-System forts, Fort Montgomery was built with three tiers. The lower level was casemated and consisted mostly of quarters and storage rooms. Only the flanks of the bastions had cannon embrasures on this lower tier. There were 20 flank howitzers mounted in the lower tier bastions. The rest of the lower-tier walls, including the entire west-facing gorge, had tall vertical rifle-slits. These were of two different designs.

The second tier, referred to in Engineer drawings and armament reports as the "Casemate Tier" was to mount 52 cannon; 32 "seacoast" guns, and 20 24-pounder flank howitzers in the bastions. The top tier, known as the "barbette", was to mount an additional 53 heavy guns.

Front II is the view most familiar to passers-by. This photo was probably taken between 1920-1924. Note the staircases still have enclosures and the dock has been taken out by ice. Clinton County Historical Association.

Front II, May 2005. It is easy to see how many layers of stone were removed from the scarp wall of the parapet.

Fronts I and II, pre-1924. This photo shows the substantial dock that adjoined the drawbridge and "water gate" at curtain I. Clinton County Historical Association.

Fronts I and II, July 1924. Ice has taken out the dock. The "water gate" can be clearly seen just north of bastion B. Photo courtesy of Judy Swink.

Fronts I and II, May 2005. Everything beyond bastion B was removed by the Weston Company in 1936-37 down to the level of the "water gate" floor. Note the significant number of trees on the parade and beyond on the coverface. Photo by the author.

Fort Montgomery as seen from the east. The top photo was taken prior to 1924 but probably after WWI. The center photo shows the results of the demolition shortly after work stopped in 1937. Two photos courtesy of Raymond Seguin. Below: The ruins in early May, 2005 during a period of very high water.

Photo by the author

14

Bastion E, curtain V at very low water. Bastion E, facing NNE, was the first bastion constructed. It was the only bastion with old-style brick embrasures at both levels. It was completely destroyed in 1936-1937. Courtesy of Clinton County Historical Association.

Photo by the author

Bastion B is still largely intact. These photos taken circa 1926, 1934 and 2002, show the bastion over the years. Note the flagstaff is not present in the earliest photo. It is not believed to have been erected by the army. 2 photos CCHA

Photo by the author

Courtesy of Clinton County Historical Association

Bastion D was left largely intact by the Weston crew. Unfortunately, it did not fare well after iron reinforcing rods were cut sometime later. A design feature of Third-System forts was that the scarp wall was detached from the rest of the structure. This caused problems with settling and in 1886 the army added iron rods to prevent the walls from collapsing outward. These walls held themselves up until the 1970's.

Photo by the author

Bastion D was unique in that it was clearly built of stone from both Isle la Motte, Vermont and King's Bay, New York. The New York stone was used early on and is found in the lower tiers of the fort. It was also lighter in color than the stone from Vermont. Bastion D collapsed into the moat in the 1970's as a result of having the iron reinforcing rods cut. Top photo from authors' collection. Bottom photos by the author May 2005.

These images show the gorge, moat and bastion C. The top photo was taken from the coverface while the recent photo was taken in November 2004 from the moat. Top: Courtesy of Raymond Seguin. Bottom: Author photo.

More views of bastion D. Ideally the photo above would not be an "exterior" view. This photo, taken in November 2004, shows what is left of the bastion from what would have been a view from the interior south down the length of the wet ditch toward the bridge.

The rare photo at left shows the same location previous to its collapse in the 1970's. Close observation of the limestone walls above the loopholes will show iron reinforcing rods, placed by the army around 1886 to prevent this sort of thing. Unfortunately, they were cut sometime after the 1930's, probably for their scrap value. This effectively assured the bastion's collapse into the moat.

Bastion C, opposite this one, the most intact part of the ruin at this time, is at risk of collapse for the same reason.

Left photo, courtesy of Raymond Seguin. Top photo by the author.

II. The Moat, Postern and Bridges

View south down the moat toward the bridge and bastion C. From a glass negative, courtesy of Powertex, Inc.

Fort Montgomery was surrounded by water on all sides. There was a wet-ditch, or moat, on the gorge (western) front purposely designed to hinder an assault by infantry. The moat stretched the full length of the gorge, 500 feet. It was 37 to 50 feet wide from scarp wall to the counterscarp wall of the coverface. The moat was 44 feet wide at the postern (entrance) to the fort. Here it was crossed by a wooden bridge. A 20 foot long, 9 foot wide drawbridge built of pine and oak rotated on an axis from a closed vertical position to meet the bridge 9 feet beyond the wall into the moat.

Photographs show at least three different variations of this bridge. All were supported on a stone column at the coverface counterscarp, while the main difference between the others consisted of the bridge supports on the fort side. Photos show one bridge supported by thick timber piles and another supported by what are clearly sawn boards. There were several different variations of the side rails also. Photos exist of the bridge with no rails, rails that extend to the drawbridge (see above), and rails that extend right to the scarp wall. We do know that this was one of the latter bridges. In later years the drawbridge was lowered to the down position and the entryway (postern) tightly boarded up.

It is not known what occasion prompted these well-dressed people to pose at the bridge across the moat. The high coverface was a popular spot for picnics and gatherings. Compare this photo with the modern-day image on the facing page for a dramatic view of how the site was changed after the Weston Company finished with their work in 1937. Photo courtesy of Raymond Seguin.

This photo, taken in May, 2005 shows how dramatically the entrance to the fort was altered. All that remains standing of the gorge is a shell with the massive supporting arches exposed. The moat was filled in at this location to allow heavy equipment entry onto the parade. It is hard to believe the location is the same. Photo by the author.

The main land entrance to the fort was by a bridge across the moat. The bridge was a popular spot for locals to gather and be photographed. This wonderful image, probably from the early 1900's, was taken after the drawbridge was lowered and the postern tightly boarded up. The photo is from the Raymond Seguin collection.

These rare photos show the 20' drawbridge and the interior doors open. We get a glimpse inside the postern and onto the parade beyond. The young man is unidentified. Bottom photo by the author shows the same location today. Top photos courtesy of Charles Barney.

These remarkable photos show the same location previous to and while the fort was being demolished. Both photos were taken from the coverface. Note in the bottom photo that the moat has no water in it and that the floors within the gorge Officer's quarter's rooms are still present. The limestone facing of the scarp wall obviously came down much easier than the massive arches. Photos courtesy of Charles Barney.

III. Interior Views- The Parade

Interior of Ft. Montgomery, Rouses Point. N.Y.

This photograph was taken across the parade toward the Northeast. We see the parade walls of Bastion E, Curtain V, and Bastion A, which projected due east. Note that many of the doors are intact and that there is even glass remaining in the windows. The supports below the casemate doors are for a catwalk. Clinton County Historical Association photo.

The parade (not parade *ground*), was relatively large at Fort Montgomery. Engineering Department plans from 1845 show the original fort (Fort "Blunder") and its significant masonry coverface sitting entirely within the bounds of the parade with plenty of room to spare. Interestingly enough, the footings for the original fort should still be there, locating and marking them would be a wonderful project for interpreters when the fort is finally preserved for future generations.

Original plans for the fort would have resulted in a much smaller parade. Plans from 1850 show that soldiers barracks were to have been constructed adjoining Curtains I and II against the south and southeast parade walls. It does appear that work may have begun on the smaller of the two barracks buildings, as indicated by photos showing limestone facing and casemate doors removed along this section of the fort.

The parade would have been a virtual hub of activity during the fort's construction. We know that during the Civil War at the height of activity, hundreds of men toiled daily at the site. Craftsmen- stonecutters, masons, carpenters and laborers of all sorts would have been set up here. Ironically, it was also here, on this massive open ground within the walls, that the Weston Company cranes and stone crusher were set up in 1936-1937. They also performed their work very well indeed.

The top photo is one of the earliest known views of the interior of the fort. It shows from left to right the parade walls of curtain V, bastion A, and curtain I. Most of the casemate doors are intact and only a few windows are broken. The lower photo shows the same view today. Top photo courtesy of Ralph Gilpin.

Top: An early view across the parade toward the NE. Visible is all of bastion E and curtain V, along with bastion A and part of curtain I. Photos of the parade wall west of bastion E are very rare. The supports visible along curtain V are for a catwalk. Bottom: The same scene post-demolition and before some of the debris was removed. Top photo courtesy of Raymond Seguin, bottom photo courtesy of Charles Barney.

Top: This photo shows the view NW across the parade toward the gorge, bastion D, and curtain IV during demolition of the fort. Note that all of the earth has been removed from the parapet of curtain IV and how floor stones from the casemates are stacked within the arches awaiting transport to the crusher just out of view to the right. Bottom: View NW from the parade, after the demolition crews had mostly finished their work. At this point curtain IV has been completely leveled but the second-story floors in the gorge Officer's quarters are still present. Photos courtesy Clinton County Historical Association (top) and Charles Barney (bottom).

Nature is slowly taking over the fort. The photo above shows the arches of the gorge and bastion D on a summer day in the early 1970's. The photo below shows the same area in early May 2004 before the vegetation was full. The vegetation is especially thick on the barbette tier of the gorge since much of the original earth from the parapet was left there by the demolition crews. Top photo courtesy of Charles Barney. Bottom photo by the author.

Another view that dramatically illustrates how nature is reclaiming the fort. The top photo is a view across the parade toward the NW in 1936 during the height of demolition work. The bottom photo shows the same scene in June 2004. Top photo: Courtesy of Clinton County Historical Association. Bottom photo by the author.

IV. Interior Views- Casemates

Fort Montgomery was a "casemated" stronghold. Casemated forts were a dramatic improvement over earlier fortifications. Prior to the development of casemates all of a fort's guns had to be placed atop fort walls, *en barbette*. The ability to place heavy guns on carriages *within* the walls of a fort dramatically increased the numbers of guns a fort could mount. Casemates were marvels of design and engineering. By utilizing strong, ingeniously designed arches, fort planners were able to construct tier upon tier, each supporting the enormous weight of the tier above it. Fort Montgomery's casemate arches were among the most difficult parts of the fort to demolish, hence we see arches standing where virtually nothing else remains.

Above: Second tier casemates of Curtain II, the front facing due south. Note the traverse circles for the Rodman guns.

Left: View west inside tier two of Bastion C. These four casemates are the only remaining "seacoast" gun emplacements remaining in the fort.

Top photo: Clinton County Historical Association. Bottom photo by the author.

Curtains I and V were built with wooden casemate floors. Plans called for their replacement but funding was not forthcoming. Photo courtesy of Powertex Corporation.

The casemates were enclosed but opened to the parade with doors and windows. This allowed for some protection from the elements and, in the case of the second-tier casemates, allowed for smoke and noise to escape when the guns were fired. The second-tier casemates were spartan, utilitarian structures. They were designed for one purpose- to enclose and support heavy guns and the men and supplies necessary to maintain them.

The lower-tier casemates, and all of the casemates in the west wall (or gorge), were actually finished rooms. These walls were constructed of brick; the rooms were finished with wood and plaster. These casemated rooms suffered from one of the most significant drawbacks of casemated forts- they were unbearably damp and dark. Heated only by fireplaces or small wood and coal stoves, life within a casemated room was uncomfortable at best.

35

The lower tier casemates resemble nothing similar to their former state. In order to get a sense of what these casemates looked like from the inside I had to travel to other Third-System forts. The top photo shows the view from within a lower tier casemate at Fort Knox in Maine. The bottom photos are of Fort Montgomery. The entire parade wall of these casemates was removed, leaving only an arch filled with debris. Plans show these rooms having kitchens, storage, and sergeant's quarters. Above left: Clinton County Historical Association photo. Top and above right: author photos.

The photo above is a close-up of the parade wall and casemates in Curtain II after doors and windows had been removed, probably just prior to demolition. The photo to the left shows the same area today. The entire upper tier has been demolished leaving only the scarp wall supporting itself. Once the parade wall and its limestone facing were removed, the massive brick arches supporting tier two became visible from the parade.

Top photo courtesy of Clinton County Historical Association. Bottom photo by the author.

10-inch Rodman's *en casemate* at Fort Jefferson. This photo could have been taken at Fort Montgomery anytime between 1872-1901. Curtain IV had seven 10-inch Rodman's mounted *en casemate* in the same manner. Directly above them, supported by enormous limestone and brick arches, stood another six guns, mounted *en barbette*. National Archives photo.

V. Interior Views- the Gorge Officer's Quarters

It is not possible to see how the Officer's Quarter's in the landward-facing west wall or gorge looked prior to demolition. No photos have come to light and it is unlikely there is anyone alive who can recall what it looked like in its prime. Once the Weston Company crews left the fort in 1937, this longest front of the fort was but a mere shell, almost unrecognizable as quarters of any kind.

We do, however, have copies of the original plans; and we can visit other Third-System forts contemporaneous to Fort Montgomery to see what these quarters looked like.

We know the Officer's Quarters were unlike any other section of the fort. Most of the fort was designed to house cannon on the second tier. The gorge was to have cannon only on the top tier; the barbette. There were over 40 rooms in the gorge on two floors. Though these rooms also were separated by massive arches built to support the guns *en barbette*, the arches were barely distinguishable inside the finished rooms.

These rooms, like those in the lower tier of the rest of the fort, were constructed of brick, most of which has been removed from the fort for reuse elsewhere. In many cases, plaster was applied directly to the brick. The second story rooms had arched ceilings where the plaster was applied to lathe, much of which is still present. Plaster still clings to some of these high ceilings.

The rooms were heated by fireplaces and wood or coal stoves. Brick alcoves were constructed for the stoves. These fireplaces are the only clues for the casual observer that these were once rooms constructed for habitation. Though many fireplaces remain, quite a few were removed for their brick. These openings leave a large gap in the arch that is easily confused for a passageway between rooms.

Without visiting similar forts it is hard to get a sense of what this section of Fort Montgomery looked like. Most of the brick has been removed and, of course, virtually all of the wood and plaster attached to it is gone.

Ruins of the gorge Officer's Quarters at Fort Montgomery. This photo clearly shows four fireplaces, two on each level. The second story floor was removed during the fort's demolition. What appears to be a passageway in the center was actually occupied by two closets, one for each room. Access to each room was by a doorway to a hallway at the parade. At top center can be seen a support for the partition between rooms, and in the distance is an enclosure for a wood or coal stove. Photo by the author.

Fort Adams, in Newport Rhode Island, and Fort Gorges in Portland, Maine, have similar quarters in the gorge sections. Fort Gorges, while deteriorating, is still relatively intact due largely to its isolated location on an island in Saco Bay. Fort Adams owes its relative state of preservation to the fact that it was utilized by the military up until the 1950's. By looking at the quarters in these forts we can get a good sense of what Fort Montgomery's Officer's Quarters looked like. Of particular note is the way plaster was sometimes applied directly to the brick, the way the rooms were partitioned, and the appearance of the hallways, doors, and windows. Plans show Fort Montgomery to have been very

40

similar in design. There are even traces of the elaborate ceiling ornamentation seen at Fort Adams clinging to what is left of the plaster ceilings at Fort Montgomery.

Quarters at Fort Adams, summer 2005. This room is probably very similar to those constructed at Fort Montgomery. These rooms have only recently been opened to the public and are to be restored. Photos by the author.

Entrance to the quarters was via a doorway at the parade wall. These doors led to a hallway that ran the width of the gorge. At the end of the hallway, at the moat side, was a narrow stairway to the second floor. The eastern and western rooms were probably divided in the center by doors that closed in the center and opened into the walls (see top photo, lower left).

41

Hallway at Fort Adams. Entrance to the quarters was by doors on either side. At Fort Montgomery, the end of the hallway culminated in a stairway to the second floor. Photo by the author.

Above: Officer's Quarters fireplace at Fort Adams.

Left: One of the fireplaces at Fort Montgomery. Almost everything that could be reused was removed from the fort prior to demolition. This included the fine wood mantles, almost all of the brick, floor boards, window frames and all of the fixtures.

Photos by the author.

Above: Detail of room adjoining the postern at Fort Gorges. Note the rifle loopholes. Top: Similar room at Fort Montgomery. This room was equipped with an enclosure for a stove rather than a fireplace. Photos by the author.

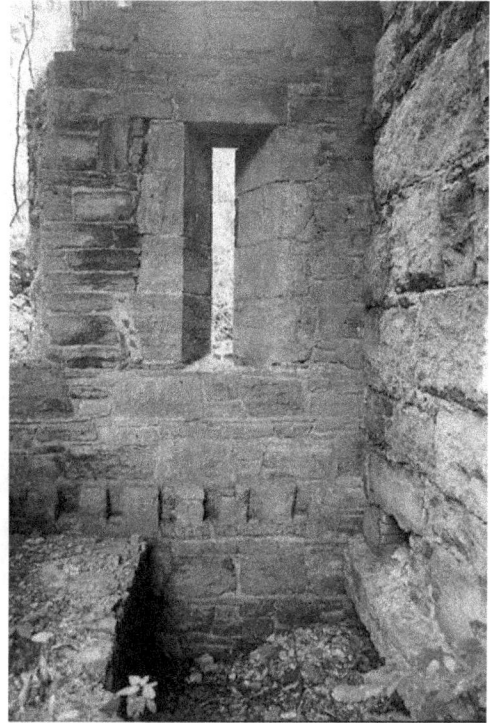

Above left: Window and rifle loophole at Fort Gorges. Above right: Similar location at Fort Montgomery. This window/loophole was smaller than most since it was located in a stairwell. By comparing the two photos we can get a good sense of how the rooms were constructed and what these interior rooms really looked like. We also get a very good idea of how much original material was removed. Below left: This photo taken at Fort Gorges shows a cross section of the interior walls. Note the plaster applied directly to the brick. Photos by the author.

The western facing scarp wall abutted the moat. Across from the moat was the massive embankment referred to in military nomenclature as the *coverface*. If an attacking enemy were to assault the fort from the west they would have to cross the forbidding wetland, endure a massive bombardment from Rodman guns atop the barbette tier and scale and descend the coverface into the moat. Once on the coverface and onto the bridge or the waters of the moat, these attackers would face a withering fire from two tiers of rifle loopholes in the scarp wall. They would also have to deal with grape and canister shot from the 24-pounder flank howitzers in the flanks of bastions C and D.

Top: Officer's quarters in the gorge at Fort Gorges in Portland, Maine. While there are differences, there are also a lot of similarities to the room below at Fort Montgomery. The photo below shows the southernmost room in the gorge, much larger than the typical room. The opening at right was not a passageway but is a fireplace with brick removed. Note that the second story scarp wall has been demolished. Photos by the author.

Top left: Ceiling ornamentation from the Officer's Quarters at Fort Adams. Top right: This is believed to be what is left of a similar feature at Fort Montgomery. Local residents who have seen these features in better condition refer to them as "chandelier bases" and maintain that lamps hung from them. Photos by the author.

Above left: First floor hallway ceiling detail in quarters at Fort Gorges. Above right: Ceiling detail of second story arched ceiling at Fort Montgomery. The lathe and even some of the plaster still clings to the limestone.

Left and above: It is hard to grasp what the interior would have looked like without having a good understanding of how it was constructed. The photo at left shows the massive stone arches at Fort Montgomery while the photo above, taken at Fort Knox in Maine, illustrates how the arches were encapsulated in brick. Photos by the author.

The gorge Officer's Quarters as seen from the parade. The southwest staircase is at the far left. Photo by the author.

VI. The Big Guns

One of the few existing photos to show mounted guns at Fort Montgomery. This view south from Canada on the Richelieu River shows a long row of 10" Rodman's mounted *en barbette*. What is not obvious are the guns mounted in casemates directly below them in curtain IV and the flank howitzers mounted in all of the bastions. Clinton County Historical Association photograph.

On December 30, 1861 Chief of Engineers Joseph G. Totten reported to New York Governor Morgan that "The new fort there placed [Rouses Point] is well advanced… it may even now resist escalade, and by the opening of the lake will be prepared to mount a number of heavy guns…Its armament will be seventy-six 10-inch guns, ten 32-pounders, forty 24-pounder howitzers, ten mortars— 136 pieces."

Totten was largely correct. Thanks largely to a Congressional appropriation of $900,000 for defenses on the northern frontier, by the end of 1872 Fort Montgomery had fully one third of its guns mounted. There was some variation in the type and number of "Columbiads" or seacoast guns, and it is not clear whether the fort ever received mortars. We do know that all 40 flank howitzers were mounted and that a number of 10-inch and 8-inch Rodman's were in position at the fort. There were also a number of older 32-pounders mounted on wooden carriages. Also present on the parade were at least two enormous 15-inch Rodman's that were planned for center-pintle mounts on the barbette. These guns were never lifted to the barbette; armament reports tell us the mounts designed to hold these huge guns were never completed.

It is clear that Fort Montgomery received 75 guns. The June 1867 Armament Report of C.E. Blunt listed the following:

➤ 7 32-pounders mounted on wooden carriages *en casemate*
➤ 10 10-inch Rodman's mounted on iron carriages *en casemate*
➤ 10 10-inch Rodman's mounted *en barbette*
➤ 8 8-inch Rodman's mounted *en barbette*
➤ 40 24-pounder flank howitzers
➤ mounted *en casemate*

With the exception of the two or three 15-inch Rodman's later on site never mounted, these numbers stayed fairly consistent. Col. Barlow's report of 1900 listed 4 32-pounders and 23 flank howitzers mounted, the number and type of Rodman's was the same.

Left and below: 10-inch Rodman mounted *en casemate* at Fort Knox in Maine. Fort Montgomery mounted 10 of these guns in casemates and another

10 *en barbette*. Photo by the author.

Above: 10-inch Rodman *en casemate* at Fort Knox in Maine. The carriage is missing a wheel used for returning the gun to firing position after recoil. Note the traverse circle beneath the wheels and the opening under the embrasure for the carriage tongue that rotates on the pintle. Left below: Collapsed casemate, bastion D, Fort Montgomery. Armament Reports show that a 10-in Rodman was mounted here. Below right: Detail, tongue and traverse circle, Fort Knox, Maine. Photos by the author.

Above: 15-inch Rodman *en barbette*, center-pintle mount at Fort Knox, Maine. Below: Location at bastion B, Fort Montgomery where a similar mount was planned but never finished. Two photos by the author.

24-pounder flank howitzers were mounted in all flanks of bastions at Fort Montgomery. The smallest guns mounted at the fort, they were anti-personnel weapons designed primarily to fire grape and canister shot at close range. This digitally enhanced photo was taken at Fort Knox, Maine. It shows two in-place flank howitzer carriages on which I have positioned the Fort Montgomery howitzer shown on the following page. Both guns are missing the traverse circles on which the small wheels would have rotated from side to side. Photo and retouching by the author.

This 24-pounder flank howitzer on display at Isle la Motte, Vermont almost certainly came from Fort Montgomery. Considering that it has sat outside for about 100 years, it is in remarkably good condition.

The Isle la Motte flank howitzer. Very few of Fort Montgomery's guns are believed to have escaped scrap metal drives during the first and second World Wars. Photo by the author.

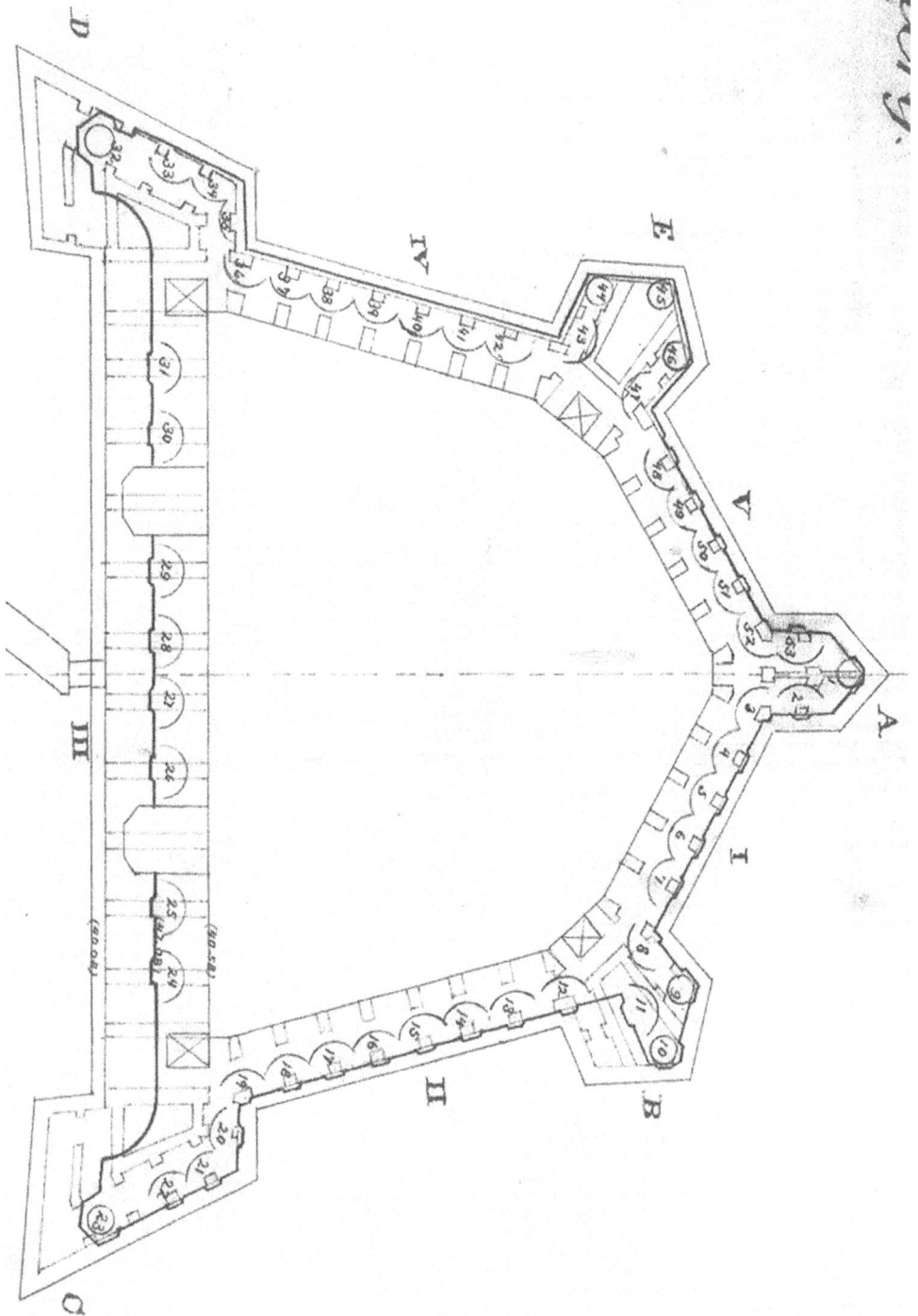

Fort Montgomery plan showing gun emplacements on the barbette. This document also shows the storage magazines in the bastions and the two service magazines on the gorge barbette. Undated, National Archives, RG 77, Drawer 7, sheet. 5a

VII. Details- The Spiral Staircases

Fort Montgomery was built over a thirty year period. Construction came in spurts, funding largely dependent upon the mood of Congress and the political situation at the time. Despite this, no expense was spared in its construction and the designers incorporated the latest in technological advances as work progressed over the years.

Detail of the barbette tier junction of front II and the gorge. This image, taken from a glass negative, provides a rare view of one of the staircase enclosures. These structures protected the staircases from the elements while allowing some light into the stone stairways. It is believed this photo was taken by caretaker Thomas Bourke. Photo courtesy of Powertex, Inc.

One of the spiral stairways at Fort Montgomery, probably the one shown above. This photo was taken after the protective enclosure was removed. Photo courtesy of Ralph Gilpin.

Among the most interesting architectural features were the spiral staircases. There were four of these stone staircases; they were located close to each of the main powder magazines. Ingeniously designed, they afforded quick access from the parade to the casemate and barbette tiers. Two were round; the others were in the shape of a semi-circle. At the top of each stairway a wooden structure was erected to protect the stairs from the elements. Two tall, vertical windows on each side let light into the dark stairway below. Photographs of these structures are quite rare, they were removed early on.

57

It is not possible to see an intact staircase at Fort Montgomery. Their fine limestone steps undoubtedly made them an easy mark for the demolition crews. Some steps remain intact at the bottom of the stairwells, while pieces of others cling precariously to the smooth sides of the remaining structures. It is obvious that most of these steps were delivered up to the gaping maw of the crusher.

Images of the southwest staircase at Fort Montgomery.

This staircase, one of two round stairways, afforded entry from the parade to the casemates and magazine in bastion C and the barbette tier of curtain II and the gorge. It was largely destroyed during the fort's demolition but is the most intact

of the four stairways. It is still possible to see the smooth sides of the walls, the notches for steps, and pieces of steps clinging to the walls in places. There are several intact steps in a pile at the bottom of the stairway. Top left: Courtesy of Ralph Gilpin, above left: courtesy of Clinton County Historical Association; above right: author photo.

58

Every smooth surface within reach is covered with graffiti. What remains of the stairways did not escape the handiwork of these "artists". These photos show the southwest staircase. Photos by the author.

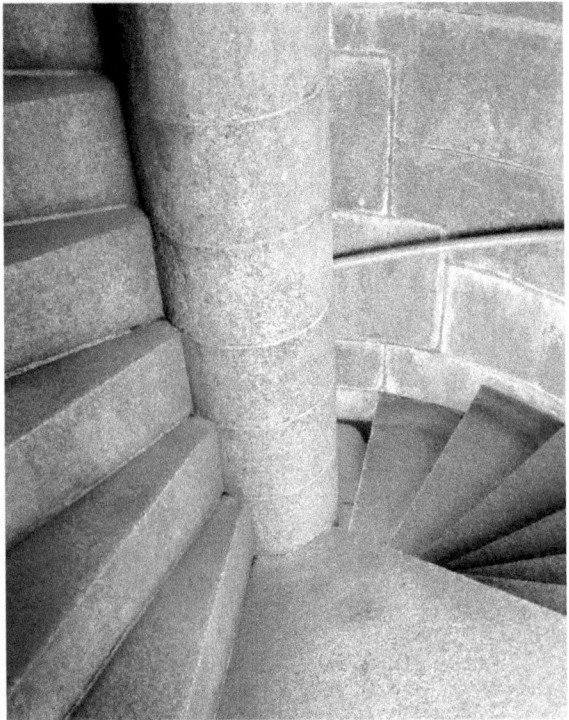

Top: The southwest staircase at Fort Montgomery. Bottom: A similar stairway at Fort Knox in Maine. Author photos.

Top and above: The northwest staircase at bastion D. Photos by the author.

The northwest staircase accessed the magazine in bastion D at Fort Montgomery. Photo by the author.

VIII. Details- Embrasures and Loopholes

Bastion C as seen through a flank howitzer embrasure in the lower tier of bastion B at Fort Montgomery. In the foreground can be seen a pintle on which the howitzer carriage would rotate. Photo by the author.

Embrasures were the reason a fort was built. Any prospective foe would have to take into account a massive stone structure pierced with dozens of ominous-looking openings from which protruded the muzzle of a Rodman gun. Fort Montgomery had 72 such embrasures opening into its casemates.

Embrasures were essential; they were also among the most vulnerable locations in a fort. Chief Engineer Totten devoted a good part of his life to perfecting embrasures; he desperately wanted an opening that would afford protection to the gun crews while providing for speed and a wide range of fire. Third-System fortifications across the country show several different variations of embrasures, many later structures have embrasures that bear Totten's name- openings with iron doors that automatically closed after firing.

Flank howitzer embrasures at the north-facing flank of bastion C allowed for firing the length of the wet ditch.

South-facing embrasure at curtain II of Fort Montgomery. This casemate was one of only three facing south that had mounted cannon. A 10-inch Rodman was mounted here as late as January 1902. Alas, this casemate was pulled down in 1936-37, leaving the scarp wall to support itself. Photos by the author.

The new-style embrasures at Fort Montgomery might very well have offered better protection from a well-placed shot. They have not, however, proven stronger than the old-style openings when it comes to surviving the elements. Most of the second tier embrasures are in very bad condition. The masonry is eroding, falling into the waters of the lake. In many places, the massive iron bands hang precariously, ready to fall. Ironically, there is one new-style embrasure, one only, that is largely intact on the outside. It faces north, towards an enemy who never came, amidst the trees and brush of collapsed bastion D. For some reason this embrasure has eroded very little. Its three iron bands are intact; it even retains the series of lines inscribed into the masonry at several angles. Several of these embrasures still have

Above: "Seacoast" gun embrasure in collapsed bastion D at Fort Montgomery. This is the best preserved new-style embrasure at the fort. Below: Iron reinforcing bands hang from a badly deteriorated embrasure at curtain II. Photos by the author.

their original pintles, especially the flank howitzer embrasures. Two remain encircled by a triangular-shaped iron piece, a remnant of the howitzer carriage that pivoted on the vertical iron rod.

All traces of the traverse irons that the carriage wheels rotated on have long disappeared, although a careful search of the floor will reveal the drill holes where they were secured to the stone. Only these pintles remain as vestiges of the great iron guns that the fort was built to enclose and support.

The lower tier of each curtain and both tiers of the gorge at Fort Montgomery were not designed to house cannon.

Above and below: Flank howitzer embrasures in bastion C at Fort Montgomery. Each retains its pintle; each at one time was the location for a 24-pounder howitzer. Two photos by the author.

These areas were reserved for housing and storage rooms. The openings onto the lake in these rooms were quite different from the large open embrasures we have examined so far. Known as "loopholes" or rifle-slits, these windows onto the lake were large, vertical slots designed to allow direct fire from within while offering some measure of protection to the fort's defenders. There were two types of these loopholes at Fort Montgomery; those along the western front, or gorge were different in design from those along the bottom tiers of the curtains facing the water.

Above: The scarp wall of bastion C showing the exterior of the loopholes. These loopholes faced west toward the moat and coverface. Below: The loopholes on the second tier as seen from within. Photos by the author.

Above: Another photo of the interior of tier two in bastion C. The entire scarp wall of bastion C along the western facing moat side consisted of tall, vertical loopholes. These openings, unlike those that were inside quarters or storage rooms, were open to the elements and were not enclosed with windows.

Left: Plans show this room in the lower tier of curtain I to have been a kitchen. This room would have been faced with brick, now removed, and finished with plaster walls and wood trim. The room was protected from the elements by glass windows much like those shown on page 45 from Fort Gorges.

Two photos by the author.

Above: This view of front II shows the embrasures of bastion C at left, and the second tier embrasures and first tier loopholes of curtain II. Notice how the loopholes are simply vertical slits and are not recessed as they are in the scarp of the gorge (below). Two photos by the author.

IX. The Barbette- Fire from the Top

Above: Intended site of a center-pintle gun mount on the barbette of bastion B. Insets: The exterior of bastion B. The scarp wall was originally much higher than it is today. Standing a full six rows of limestone above the cordon, it would have provided a measure of protection to gun crews at this battery. Below left: A center-pintle barbette mount at Fort Knox, Maine. Three photos by the author. Inset photo above courtesy Clinton County Historical Association.

The barbette of Fort Montgomery was designed to mount 53 heavy guns. The casemates below were intended to mount a total of 72 guns, but 20 of those were the much smaller flank howitzers. Thus the barbette tier was intended to be a very formidable part of this fort's defensive strategy.

The barbette armament was to feature some of the army's biggest guns.

Included in the plans for the barbette's 53 gun mounts were 8 center-pintle mounts. One was to be placed at the salient of eastern-pointing bastion A, two at bastion B, one each at bastions C and D, and three atop bastion E, the salient of which pointed directly at Quebec. While plans appear to show these circular mounts were originally designed to hold 10-inch Rodman's we know at least 2 of the monster 15-inch guns were on site (but not mounted) for years. These huge guns would have required a much more sophisticated mount than the one shown on the previous page (page 52 shows a mounted 15-inch Rodman at Fort Knox).

Fore-pintle mounts dominated the barbette of Fort Montgomery. The February 1, 1872 Armament Report plan shows 2 fore-pintle mounted 8-inch Rodman's on bastion A. The sole center-pintle mount was not complete. Curtain I had 5 fore-pintle mounts, all of which were "ready for Guns." Bastion B- 2 fore-pintle mounts, one hosted another 8-inch Rodman. The 2 center-pintle mounts were not complete, the "traverse circles on hand, but not yet laid." Curtain II was to hold 8 fore-pintle mounted guns, of which 7 were "ready for Guns." Bastion C was intended for 3 fore-pintle mounted guns and 1 center-pintle mounted Rodman. The center-pintle mount and another fore-pintle were "not commenced." The barbette tier was especially important at the western-facing gorge (curtain III) since there were no casemated guns. Here were mounted 4 8-inch Rodman's. Of the 4 southernmost mounts- two were "ready for Guns", and two were "not commenced."

Fore-pintle barbette mount at Fort Knox, Maine. This mount is virtually identical to those used at Fort Montgomery. Note the mount still retains its pintle and traverse circles. Photo by the author.

Pintles were the iron posts that a gun carriage rotated around. Above: Vintage photo of a barbette mount pintle with intact pin at Fort Montgomery. It is not known if this pintle is still present. Left, recent photo of a pintle on the bastion B barbette. The pin has been removed. Top photo courtesy of Raymond Seguin, left, by the author.

Also on the gorge barbette were two service magazines. It is unclear as to if they were ever finished. What is left of them may still be seen deep within the thick undergrowth atop the gorge.

The northwest bastion- bastion D- mounted some serious ordnance. Four guns were planned here- three of them were mounted, all 10-inch Rodman's. The one center-pintle mount never received its traverse circles. North-facing curtain IV was the only one to receive its full complement of guns; the barbette here bristled with 7 10-inch Rodman's. Bastion E was to have an unusual three center-pintle mounted guns together with 2 fore-pintle mounts. One 8-inch Rodman was mounted here in 1872. Finally, curtain V was to mount 5 guns on fore-pintle mounts. None were placed here.

Above: Fore-pintle mounts on the barbette at Fort Knox, Maine. The barbette tiers on the curtains of Fort Montgomery would have looked very similar to this. Below: The scarp of south-facing curtain II at Ft. Montgomery. Several rows of limestone were removed from atop this wall by the demolition crews in 1936-37. Most of the barbette has been destroyed as have been the bulk of the second-tier casemates below. By design, the outward-facing scarp wall was not connected to the rest of the parapet. When the casemate tier below was demolished this wall was left free standing, with nothing behind it.

Two views of the scarp wall of curtain II, the wall visible from the Rouses Point Bridge. The barbette is no longer present here, having been removed in 1936-1937. Photos by the author.

X. People- Fort Montgomery and the Locals

This photo dated 1916 shows a trio of young people on the gorge barbette. Courtesy of Raymond Seguin.

Local people have always been rather possessive about "their" fort. This might seem surprising in the light of its being delivered up to the cranes and crusher of the Weston Company in 1936. As many an elderly resident will gladly share, those were different times, unusual times. Those were the dark days of the Great Depression. To many a local resident, nostalgia for "Fort Blunder" was of necessity trumped by the promise of jobs and the prosperity to come with a great new bridge across the lake.

Yet, Fort Montgomery has held local folks in its spell from its earliest days till the present.

There are few photos of the interior of Fort Montgomery that have come to light, yet many wonderful photos have surfaced of people at different locations on and around the fort. One of the favorite locations was the massive coverface. Here, on this huge man-made island, just to the east of the "commons", local folks would come to play, picnic, court and explore. Just over the rise was the mysterious moat, with its bridge to the fort, culminating in an entrance (postern) long boarded up for most visitors. Yet, we know enterprising local people did enter the fort, we have fascinating photos of them on the parade, high on the barbette, peering through the embrasures (from the inside) and, in one instance, we even have a snapshot of a woman entering the fort thorough an embrasure in the moat (see page 7). We know there was an ill-fated attempt to use the fort as a campground. This effort by an otherwise successful local entrepreneur was ahead of its time and failed. Yet, in later years Boy Scout Camporees were held on the grounds, rather surprising considering the risk of injury to the young scouts.

Above: Two young women, identified as "Aunts Lillie and Edith" by Ruth Seguin, sit atop the coverface north of the fort. Below: The same women explore the bridge between the coverface and the tightly boarded up main entrance (or postern) to the fort. Photos courtesy of Raymond Seguin and Ruth Seguin.

Even after the fort was demolished, local people found its allure irresistible. Much to the chagrin of property owners, trespassing on the grounds did not stop when the Weston Company crews left the massive edifice but a mere shadow of its former self in 1937. Unfortunately the opposite occurred, young people came in droves to the site, some to play and explore dark and forbidden places; others, all too often, to party, vandalize and cart off what the wreckers left behind. It appears that for every individual with permission to be at the ruins, many others were simply trespassing, oftentimes in groups to party or vandalize the ruins. Photos show layer upon layer of graffiti accumulated over the years.

Those who took the time to ask permission to visit the ruins, and who showed proper respect and care for the fragile walls and understood the potential danger, were usually granted the opportunity to visit. Only recently, when the ruins simply became too dangerous, and a litigious public forced serious liability concerns upon the current owners was the "No Trespassing" rule strictly enforced. This writer was granted unprecedented access to the fort, but only after establishing a good relationship with the owners and promising that, along with telling the story, I would make sure people understood they could not visit the fort in its current condition. I was also required to sign a waiver of liability should I be injured on the grounds.

Things are different at Fort Montgomery today; for a variety of reasons. On almost every research trip I have made to the site, I have been stopped by law enforcement personnel. Local police, State Police, Customs and Immigration Agents and now, Homeland Security people regularly patrol the grounds. In talking with these law enforcement officers, I was astounded to hear of the number of arrests that have been made. The property is clearly posted. It is an unfortunate but necessary fact of life that Fort Montgomery will have to stay "off limits" until it passes from private ownership to the stewardship of a public entity. The current owners cannot be faulted; their present course is the prudent, responsible one.

Lack of access has not diminished interest in the grand old fort, however.

Early automobiles atop the barbette and within the passageway to the bridge at Fort Montgomery. Photo courtesy of Raymond Seguin.

In the few short years this writer has been researching the fort extensively, I have given several presentations about the fort, mostly at the invitation of local historical societies and museums. Each was very well attended, one July evening in Isle la Motte an overflow crowd of over a hundred packed the local elementary school cafeteria, remarkable for a hot summer night in rural Vermont. The old fort just south of the border continues to fascinate and intrigue.

Above: A young couple on the top of the coverface south of the fort. Below: A woman and young boy on the coverface just south of the bridge. Photos courtesy of Raymond Seguin.

Above left: Charles Barney and Stanley Monette atop the barbette, early 1930's. Above right: An outing on the parade at Fort Montgomery. Left: Charles Fitch "flagpole sitting", 1933. Three photos courtesy of Charles Barney.

Left: An unidentified young couple sits together high atop the coverface at Fort Montgomery. Photo courtesy of Raymond Seguin.

Below: Young people pose at the boarded up postern and on the bridge over the moat. Two photos from the author's collection.

A Boy Scout group leaves the fort grounds, probably in the 1950's. Photo courtesy of Silva Mary Mames.

Fort Montgomery UDI detail - May 24, 2002

Above: Public safety officials pose at Fort Montgomery. The group consists of members of the US Coast Guard, New York State Police, Grand Isle County Vermont Sheriff's Department, Clinton County New York Sheriff's Department and Rouses Point New York Police Department. Top photo provided by Lieutenant Todd A. St. Louis, New York State Police. Below: Law enforcement officials check to make sure we have permission to be on site. Author photo.

Clinton County Historical Association President Roger Harwood has been a big supporter of Fort Montgomery. My friend and colleague, his efforts were instrumental in supporting my ongoing research at the fort. In the photo above Roger Harwood takes WCAX reporter Jack LaDuke back to his vehicle on the Vermont shore after an interview. Below: Roger Harwood at work mowing the parade at Fort Montgomery. Photos by the author.

Local television stations have recognized the public's interest in Fort Montgomery and have provided excellent coverage. WPTZ's Thom Hallock and Mike French toured the fort with the author to prepare a joint Lake Champlain Basin Program/WPTZ "Champlain 2000" segment. WCAX's Jack LaDuke toured the fort and interviewed the author on site in 2004. Photos by the author.

XI. Aerial Photos

Fort Montgomery can be seen in the lower left of this photo. At the very bottom is the second Rouses Point Bridge, built to replace the one that utilized stone from the fort. In the distance is Quebec; Ash Island is the closest island in the river, Isle aux Noix can be seen in the distance at the bend in the river. Beyond are Chambly, Montreal, and the mighty Saint Lawrence River. Photo courtesy of Roger and Doug Harwood.

Few photos can show the strategic location and illustrate the changes to the fort over the years better than aerial images. Thanks to the hard work and generosity of Doug and Roger Harwood I have been able to share a perspective on the ruins that few others have experienced. Many of these wonderful photos are featured on the next several pages

When one considers the location of the fort and the long military history of the lake, it seems remarkable that Island Point was not fortified sooner than it was. We know there was talk of erecting works at Rouses Point as early as the Revolution, yet it appears nothing of significance occurred until 1816 when Totten began construction of the ill-fated "Fort Blunder".

Aerial photos show the massive stone fort well within the waters of the lake occupying an entire island, the opposite shoreline well within reach of its heavy guns.

Just beyond, a few hundred yards to the north down the Richelieu, lays Canada. It is from here an enemy would come, just as they had numerous times in the past. Students of history understand, however, that invading forces also sailed north, up the mighty river. This massive fort could also be used as a staging area for an American invasion, a possibility not lost on British and Canadian military strategists. Fort Lennox, situated on Isle aux Noix, just beyond the bend of the river, bears mute testimony to that fear.

Fort Lennox at Isle aux Noix was built as a reaction to American fortifications at Rouses Point. The fort, a National Historic Site, is in remarkable condition and is a marvelous example of how a fort can and should be preserved. Fort Lennox is well-maintained and staffed by an outstanding group of interpreters. Both Fort Montgomery and Fort Lennox were constructed of limestone from Fisk quarry in Isle la Motte, Vermont. Aerial photos courtesy of Roger and Doug Harwood. Bottom right: Author photo.

Fort Montgomery, the "commons", and Rouses Point from the air, April 2005. The top photo provides an excellent view of the adjacent property, once know as the Fort Montgomery Military Reservation. The "point" at Rouses Point is located almost exactly under the once disputed 42nd parallel. It was here the earliest settlers built their homes. The point can be seen at the location where the bridge meets the mainland. The bottom photo was taken from the Vermont side. Two photos courtesy of Doug and Roger Harwood.

April 2005

May 2002

When researching the fort, it was important to try to get the island before the vegetation became lush. We spent many cold days at the fort in April and November. These aerial photographs dramatically illustrate the difference a month can make here in the North Country. Courtesy of Doug and Roger Harwood.

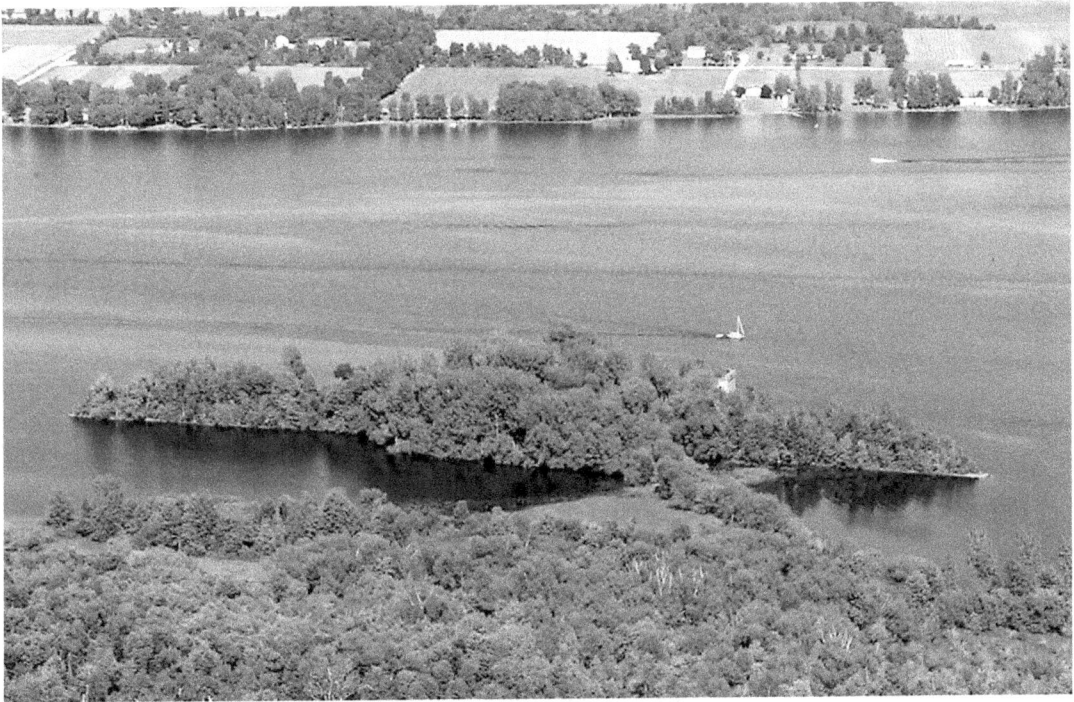

Above: Island Point as seen from the west over the "commons" in the summer of 2004. Note how lush the vegetation is. During the fort's active life, the coverface would have been kept mowed, the grass closely cropped. Below: View toward the west, April 2005. The water is high at this date but has been known to get much higher than this. Two aerial photos courtesy of Doug and Roger Harwood.

Fort Montgomery ruins, April 2005. Photo courtesy of Roger and Doug Harwood.

The Future: What lies ahead?

Fort Montgomery, despite all of the interest it has generated among the local populace, has not fared well over the years. This great stone edifice that moved Daniel Taylor to write so glowingly about it during the 1890's has suffered one indignity after another through the years.

Studying as I have the plans, letters and other documents created by the fort's builders over the years, it has been difficult not to become attached to this great old structure. I have come to respect the engineers, craftsmen, and officials who were involved in its design, construction and maintenance. Many of these men worked on this fort for the full thirty years it was under construction. I have many of their names; I have discovered what their particular skill or task was. They were all essential, the Chief Engineer, the mason, the carpenter, the stonecutter, the laborer and the teamster. They all left a part of themselves in Fort Montgomery.

The story of Fort Montgomery is not only a tale of brick and stone. It is not solely about political developments or military history. It is also a tale of everyday people, the men who toiled at Island Point day after day, week after week. It has been an honor to learn about them; it will be a privilege to write of them in detail in the book to follow.

It will take time to tell the story well, to relate the story in the detail it deserves. This book was necessary too, however. Time is of the essence. Few are alive today who remember the fort before it was demolished. I have sought out those I could find, yes, to see if they had photographs or memorabilia to share. But also so they might share their memories, anecdotes and experiences.

Many of their photos are reproduced here in this little book. I am anxious to be able to share their precious images with the world. I would like this book to be available to these men and women so they and their loved ones might see their photos in print. I also want them to be able to discover what I have learned about that special place they recall from so long ago.

Time is also of the essence in that the ruins at Island Point need attention. I believe the ruins are in grave danger of further collapse. The most intact portion of the fort, the great bastion to the southwest, remains very much like it was when constructed.

Without reinforcement in the form of replacing the steel rods that were removed sometime after the 1930's, however, it is my concern that these walls will suffer the same fate as their mirror image to the northwest. That bastion collapsed into the moat some time during the 1970's or early 1980's. This must not be allowed to happen.

The current owners of the property cannot be expected to shore up the ruins. They have tried in the past to see to it that this important historic site, a site that is listed on the National Register of Historic Places, was turned over to responsible state or local entities. The late Victor Podd was willing to give the fort to New York State at one time. The offer was declined. The property is for sale once again.

The current owners deserve a return on their investment. Island Point is but a small part of the property formerly known as the Fort Montgomery Military Reservation, now Fort Montgomery Estates. It is my belief that they are willing to work with responsible government agencies and civic groups regarding the ruins on their property. Much attention has been given the fort in the media of late. It is my hope that this book, and the one to follow, will help keep that attention and interest alive.

I do not believe the fort will ever be restored. I don't think it is reasonable, it may not be possible. It should however, be cleaned up and made safe and publicly accessible. Ironically, the demolition that took place in the 1930's actually helps in a way to make the fort easily "interpretable". A preserved Fort Montgomery would be a boon to the local economy. It would bring tourists and history buffs from everywhere to the Rouses Point area. Most importantly it would preserve an important part of our heritage on this most historic waterway.

Fort Montgomery, and the hundreds of men who toiled there over the decades, deserve nothing less.

Glossary

Barbette

The uppermost tier or level of a fort, usually without any overhead protection.

Bastion

A projection between the straight, recessed sections of a fort known as curtains. Fort Montgomery had five bastions, labeled clockwise from the east bastion A-E.

Battery

A position for a gun or group of guns within a fort.

Canister

An anti-personnel weapon consisting of containers filled with iron balls (or shot). When fired, the container splits open filling the air with the small projectiles much like a shotgun.

Casemate

A masonry vault specifically designed to be bombproof usually constructed under the ramparts of a fort. Casemates usually housed cannon, but they were also designed to protect and enclose quarters, storerooms, kitchens and other general purpose rooms.

Cordon

An outward projection from the scarp wall near the top. The main purpose of the cordon was to help reduce weathering due to drainage. It may have also been considered an obstacle to scaling the wall.

Counterscarp

The wall of the wet ditch or moat opposite the main work. At Fort Montgomery this was the coverface wall directly opposite the gorge, or western wall.

Coverface

An earth or masonry outwork placed to protect a masonry front of a fort from siege guns. At Fort Montgomery the coverface was a huge artificial island constructed between the gorge, or western front, and the western shore.

Curtain

The straight sections of a fort that lie between two bastions. Fort Montgomery had five curtains, numbered clockwise from the SE curtain I-V.

Embrasure

An opening in the wall through which guns are fired.

En barbette

A gun mounted on a barbette or top tier of the fort. These guns would fire over the wall rather than through an embrasure.

En casemate

A gun mounted in a casemate. Guns mounted en casemate would fire through an opening or embrasure in the scarp.

Flank howitzer

A smaller gun specially designed as an anti-personnel weapon. Flank howitzers were placed in the flanks of the bastions and were primarily designed to fire grapeshot or canister.

Front

The exterior portion of a fort between the salients of two bastions. Fort Montgomery had five fronts.

Gorge

The front of a fort facing away from the water, usually where the main entrance to the fort was located. At Fort Montgomery the gorge was the westward-facing side, toward the coverface and "commons."

Loophole

A narrow opening or embrasure designed to allow the defenders to fire small arms from within.

Magazine

Storage room for gun powder. There were two types of magazines at Fort Montgomery. Four main storage magazines deep within bastions B-E and two smaller service magazines atop the gorge barbette.

Moat, aka Wet Ditch

A low area around a scarp wall designed to prevent troops from accessing the fort wall.

Parade

The open space within the fort, often used for barracks, drilling and assembling, etc. In Third-System forts this open area was not referred to as a parade *ground*.

Parade wall or face

The interior wall of the rampart facing the parade.

Parapet

A low earth or masonry wall along the top of the rampart over which defenders would fire their weapons.

Pintle

An upright iron pin upon which a gun chassis rotates.

Postern

The entrance from a fort toward the moat or ditch. At Fort Montgomery the postern was the entryway to the fort from the west, across the moat, through the gorge.

Rampart

The main body of fort wall from scarp to parade.

Salient

The outward-pointing angle of a bastion.

Sally Port

A postern, usually the main entrance to the fort located in the gorge.

Scarp, scarp wall

The exterior wall immediately in front of the rampart along the perimeter. Third-System scarp walls were by design unattached to the rest of the rampart.

Shell

A hollow projectile usually filled with explosives.

Shot

A solid projectile made of iron.

Traverse circle or iron

An arc of stone or iron upon which the wheels of a gun chassis rotated.

About the author

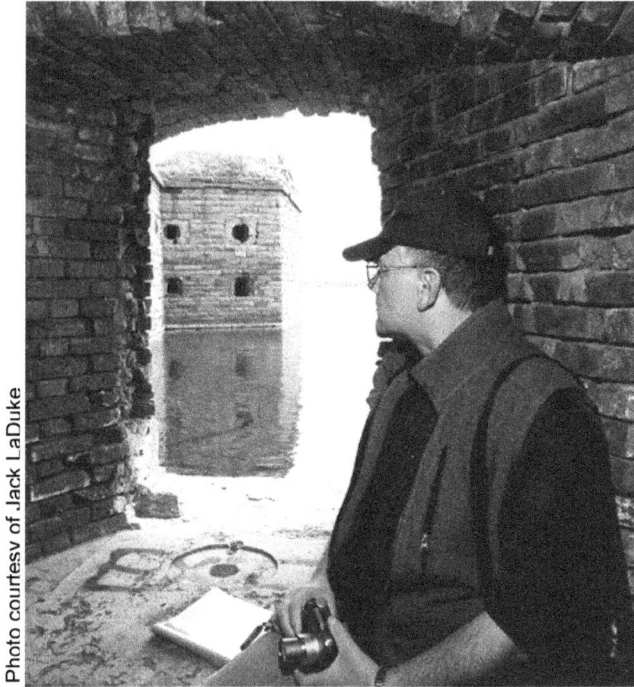

Jim Millard is the publisher of the award-winning America's Historic Lakes website and the author of "The Secrets of Crab Island" and several articles about the history of the Lake Champlain and Lake George region.

Through the America's Historic Lakes project, Jim has provided materials for use in atlases, encyclopedias, public television documentaries and educational textbooks.

His next book will be a comprehensive history of the all of the fortifications in the Rouses Point area; Fort "Blunder", Fort Montgomery, and the never constructed fortifications planned for Stony Point and Windmill Point, Vermont.

Jim is a member of the Vermont Historical Society, Clinton County Historical Association, Mount Independence Coalition, and the American Association for State and Local History. Jim has been the webmaster for the Valcour Bay Research Project since its inception and he maintains the website for the Clinton County Historical Association in Plattsburgh, New York.

He is employed by Saint Michael's College, as a Senior Instructional Support Specialist with the Information Technology Department. Jim lives with his wife, Lynn, on the western shore of Lake Champlain. They have six grown children and six grandchildren.

www.ingramcontent.com/pod-product-compliance
Lightning Source LLC
Chambersburg PA
CBHW062106090426
42741CB00015B/3341